ISBN 978-1-332-26611-1
PIBN 10306474

For support please visit www.forgottenbooks.com

1 MONTH OF
FREE
READING

at
www.ForgottenBooks.com

By purchasing this book you are eligible for one month membership to ForgottenBooks.com, giving you unlimited access to our entire collection of over 700,000 titles via our web site and mobile apps.

To claim your free month visit:
www.forgottenbooks.com/free306474

Similar Books Are Available from
www.forgottenbooks.com

Intertemporal Substitution in Macroeconomics

N. Gregory Mankiw
Julio J. Rotemberg
Lawrence H. Summers

April 1982
Revised May 1982

Working Paper #1319-82

Intertemporal Substitution in Macroeconomics

N. Gregory Mankiw
Julio J. Rotemberg
Lawrence H. Summers

April 1982
Revised May 1982

Working Paper #1319-82

INTERTEMPORAL SUBSTITUTION IN MACROECONOMICS

by

N. Gregory Mankiw*
Julio J. Rotemberg**
Lawrence H. Summers**

April 1982
Revised May 1982

*Massachusetts Institute of Technology and Harvard Law School
**Massachusetts Institute of Technology and NBER

We are grateful to David Runkle for his research assistance and to Henry Farber, Robert Shiller and Laurence Weiss for helpful comments.

0744943

INTERTEMPORAL SUBSTITUTION IN MACROECONOMICS

ABSTRACT

Modern neoclassical theories of the business cycle posit that aggregate fluctuations in consumption and employment are the consequence of dynamic optimizing behavior by economic agents who face no quantity constraint. In this paper, we estimate an explicit model of this type. In particular, we assume that the observed fluctuations correspond to the decisions of an optimizing representative individual. This individual has a stable utility function which is additively separable over time but not necessarily additively separable in consumption and leisure. We estimate three first order conditions which represent three margins on which the individual is optimizing. He can trade off present consumption for future consumption, present leisure for future leisure and present consumption for present leisure. Our results show that the aggregate U.S. data are extremely reluctant to be characterized by a model of this type. Not only are the overidentifying restrictions statistically rejected but, in addition, the estimated utility function is often not concave. Even when it is concave the estimates imply that either consumption or leisure is an inferior good.

I. INTRODUCTION

Modern neoclassical theories of the business cycle are founded upon
the assumption that fluctuations in consumption and employment are the
consequence of dynamic optimizing behavior by economic agents who face no
quantity constraints. In this paper, we present and estimate an explicit
operational model of an optimizing household. Our examination of post-
war aggregate data provides no support for these theories.

As in many recent studies of consumption and asset returns, we posit
that observed fluctuations can be modeled as the outcome of optimizing
decisions of a representative individual. The individual has a utility
function that is additively separable through time and faces an economic
environment where future opportunities are uncertain. Our approach
avoids the intractable problem of finding a closed form solution for the
representative individual's choices. Rather, we use the restrictions on
the data implied by the first-order conditions for an optimum. The
estimation of these first-order conditions makes it possible to recover
the structural parameters of the underlying utility function.

The three first-order conditions we consider represent three margins
on which the representative individual is optimizing. He can trade-off
present and future consumption at a stochastic real interest rate
measured in terms of the consumption good. He can trade-off present
leisure and future leisure at a stochastic real interest rate measured in
terms of leisure. And he can trade-off present consumption and present
leisure at the real wage. Thus the approach taken here has the potential

to recover parameters describing both consumption and labor supply decisions.

The estimation technique we use is the nonlinear instrumental variables procedure Hansen and Singleton (1981) suggest. It not only produces consistent estimates of the relevant parameters, but also allows us to test overidentifying restrictions implied by the theory. Throughout the study, we experiment with different measures of consumption, different lists of instruments, and different frequency data. We also try various functional forms for the underlying utility function. In particular, we allow the utility function to be non-separable in consumption and leisure. Such experimentation assures our conclusions are robust to changes in the various auxiliary assumptions necessary for implementation of the model.

We find that aggregate data is not readily characterized as ex post realizations from a stochastic dynamic optimization. In particular, the orthogonality conditions implied by theory are almost always rejected. More importantly, the parameter estimates are usually highly implausible. The estimated utility function is often not concave, which implies that the representative individual is not at a maximum of utility, but at a saddle-point or at a minimum. In addition, the estimates imply that either consumption or leisure is an inferior good. We conclude that observed economic fluctuations do not easily admit of a neoclassical interpretation.

Section II discusses the previous work on intertemporal substitution. Section III develops the model, while Section IV discusses the

data. Section V explains the estimation procedure, and section VI
presents the results. Section VI considers the implications of the
model's failure for equilibrium theories of the business cycle, and
suggests directions for future research.

II. MOTIVATION

The major difference between modern neoclassical and traditional
Keynesian macro-economic theories is that the former regard observed
levels of employment, consumption and output as realizations from dynamic
optimizing decisions by both households and firms, while the latter
regard them as reflecting constraints on firms and households. This
distinction is clearest in the case of labor supply decisions. In
classical macro-economic models, observed levels of labor supply
represent the optimizing choices of households given their perceptions of
the macro-economic environment. In Keynesian macro-models, employment is
frequently regarded as "demand determined" and fluctuations in employment
do not necessarily correspond to any change in desired labor supply.

The goal of the present paper is to examine the extent to which data
on consumption and labor supply for the United States over the post-war
period are consistent with the hypothesis of continuous dynamic optimization. At the outset, it is crucial to be clear about the limitations of
this empirical inquiry, or any investigation of this kind. It is
impossible to test the general proposition about continuous optimization
discussed above. Only particular simple versions of the dynamic

optimization problem can be considered. Any rejections of the models
estimated can be interpreted as a failure of the underlying theory or of
the particular parametrization of it which is tested. Of course, to the
extent that a theory fails when simply expressed, its utility as an
organizing framework for understanding economic events is called into
question.

Explanations of business cycles based on continuous dynamic
optimization differ in many respects. However, they share the notion
that the elasticity of labor supply with respect to changes in the
relative return from working currently and in the near future is likely
to be quite high. This would seem to be a necessary implication of any
such theory, since cyclical fluctuations in employment are large and the
long-run labor supply elasticity observed in cross-sections is typically
small. A central thrust of this paper is to examine empirically the
differential response of labor supply to permanent and transitory shocks
to real wages.

Recent research on consumption by Grossman and Shiller (1981),
Hansen and Singleton (1981), Hall (1978, 1981) and Mankiw (1981) shows
how it is possible to estimate directly the parameters of the
intertemporal utility function characterizing the behavior of the
representative individual. Hansen and Singleton (1981) and Mankiw (1981)
show how to test the overidentifying restrictions that are implied by the
hypothesis of continuous optimization of a stable additively separable
utility function. The major virtue of the approach pioneered by these
authors is that it permits utility function parameters to be estimated

directly without requiring explicit solutions of the consumers' dynamic optimization problem. Unfortunately, both Hansen and Singleton and Mankiw report rejections of their estimated models.

This paper uses techniques similar to those developed in connection with consumption to estimate the parameters of an intertemporal utility function characterizing the labor supply behavior of the representative consumer. This permits judgements to be made about the magnitude of the key intertemporal elasticities. In addition, we can directly test the hypothesis of dynamic optimization using the implied overidentifying restrictions on the data. A major additional motivation for this research is the rejection of the overidentifying restrictions in the models Hansen and Singleton (1981) and Mankiw (1981) estimate. These models all maintain the assumption that the marginal utility of consumption depends only on the level of consumption. It is natural to entertain the hypothesis that the utility function is not separable so that the marginal utility of consumption depends on the level of leisure. The intertemporal utility functions we estimate allow this possibility.

There are at least two other motivations for estimating an intertemporal utility function characterizing the behavior of both consumption and leisure. As Feldstein (1978) demonstrates, the form of this utility function determines the optimal structure of consumption and income taxation. If consumption and leisure are additively separable, optimal taxation involves a zero tax rate on capital income. More generally, depending on the relative substitutability of present and future consumption with leisure, a negative or positive tax rate on capital income is appropriate. While the absence of empirical evidence on these crucial cross-effects has been widely noted, no empirical estimates of the full intertemporal utility function are yet available.

A second motivation for exploring intertemporal substitutability of consumption and leisure is provided by models of the business cycle based on imperfect information. These models which date from the contribution of Lucas (1973) have in common a Lucas supply function of the form:

$$y = \alpha_0 + \alpha_1 (p-p^e) \qquad \alpha_1 > 0 \tag{1}$$

This supply function states that when prices are unexpectedly high, producers capitalize on their perceived transitory opportunity and produce more output. While there is no logical flaw in this argument, Friedman (1980) and Barro (1980) point out an equally compelling argument in the opposite direction. When prices are transitorily high, the demand for output should be low as consumers substitute their consumption towards periods when output is less costly. Hence the sign of the correlation between unexpected price shocks and output is theoretically ambiguous. The validity of (1) as a reduced form description of macroeconomic behavior depends on its implicit premise that aggregate supply is more responsive to transitory shocks than is aggregate demand. Comparison of the estimated intertemporal substitutability of consumption and leisure can throw light on this issue.

Several previous papers attempt to measure the extent of intertemporal substitution in labor supply using aggregate data. These papers do not try to estimate directly the parameters of an underlying utility function but attempt to estimate structural labor supply equations. The results are mixed. Lucas and Rapping (1969) provide estimates of an aggregate labor supply function which suggest very large intertemporal substitution effects. Their results depend on the Koyck lag-adaptive expectations scheme they use to model expectations of future wages and prices. Altonji (1981) shows that when the Lucas-Rapping equations are re-estimated using several different econometric techniques to proxy rational expectations, the results are almost invariably inconsistent with the intertemporal substitution hypothesis. Clark and Summers (1982) also report econometric evidence inconsistent with the substitution hypothesis, drawing on both aggregate time series and information on local labor markets.

In an influential recent paper, Hall (1980) obtains estimates which he views as providing support for the intertemporal substitution hypothesis. However, it is very difficult to interpret his econometric formulation. The labor supply equation that Hall estimates is of the form:

$$L_t^s = \alpha + \beta \ (w_t + r_t) \tag{2}$$

where w_t is the log of the real wage, and r_t is the real interest rate.

The motivation for this specification is unclear. The intertemporal substitution hypothesis implies that labor supply should depend on the relative return from working in period t and from working in period t+1. This depends on the real wage in period t relative to the discounted real wage in period t+1. The omission of expected future real wages from (2) makes it hard to interpret the resulting estimates.

These studies of intertemporal substitution share two major difficulties. The first is the question of identification. Since the labor supply schedule is likely to shift through time, it is inappropriate to regard the real wage as an exogenous variable. The problem is that satisfactory instruments are almost impossible to find. Labor supply shocks are likely to affect most macroeconomic policy variables. After a lengthy discussion of the pitfalls to be avoided in selecting instruments for the estimation of (2), Hall settles on measures of military spending as exogenous determinants of aggregate demand. But, military spending is highly correlated with the size of the draft which has a direct impact on labor supply. The problem of finding suitable instruments becomes even more formidable when the supply equations include expectational variables.

The second difficulty involves the measurement of expectations. The theory holds that labor supply should be a function of the distribution of the entire path of future real wages and interest rates, not just of the first moments of those variables in the succeeding period. Satisfactory proxies for these expectations are almost impossible to develop. Problems of serial correlation and the length of the expectational horizon rule out the possibility of using instrumental variable procedures of the type McCallum (1976) suggests to solve this problem.

Hence, there is very little empirical evidence at the aggregate level bearing on the importance of the intertemporal substitution effects upon which modern neoclassical macroeconomics models are premised. In recent papers, MaCurdy (1981a,b) examines intertemporal substitution effects at the micro-econometric level. It might at first seem that micro data provide a much firmer basis for estimating intertemporal substitution effects than do aggregate data. However, the use of micro data involves serious problems. At the micro level, wages and changes in wages are typically taken as exogenous. It is difficult to justify this assumption. Individual wages presumably differ because of differences in individual characteristics which affect their productivity. It is difficult to see why these same characteristics-motivation, innate ability or whatever-should not also be associated with the taste for working.

III. THEORY

This section describes the model to be estimated. To estimate the model, it is necessary to make a number of auxiliary assumptions about the behavior of consumers. These assumptions pertain to issues such as the information set available to consumers and the functional form of their utility functions. Tests of the model are also tests of these

auxiliary assumptions, so they require careful attention. We make a
major effort to explore alternative sets of auxiliary assumptions to
insure the robustness of our conclusion regarding the economic issues of
major interest.

We examine a basic premise of many classical macro-economic models
that observed movements in per capita consumption and leisure correspond
to the behavior of a rational individual who derives pleasure from these
two goods and whose utility function is additively separable over time[1]
and is stationary. Such a utility function is:

$$V_t = E_t \sum_{\tau=t} \rho^{\tau-t} U(C_\tau, L_\tau) \tag{3}$$

Here, V_t is expected utility at t, E_t is the expectations operator
conditional on information available at t, ρ is a constant discount
factor, C_τ is consumption of goods at τ, L_τ is leisure at τ and U is a
function which is increasing and concave in its two arguments.

Given a specification of the budget constraint, and of the
conditional distributions of all future wages, prices and rates of return
an all assets, it would in principle be possible to use (3) to find

---

[1]The models of Lucas and Rapping (1970), Prescott and Mehra (1980),
Long and Flosser (1980) and King and Flosser (1981) for example exhibit
this feature. Some models such as those of Kydland and Prescott (1979)
rely on the absence of additive separability to generate intertemporal
substitution effects. We return to this possibility in the final section
of the paper.

consumers' choices of consumption and leisure at time t. In practice it
is almost impossible to conceive of all this information being available
to the econometrician. Even were it available, analytical solutions of
(3) do not exist even for very simple functional forms. Therefore,
following earlier work on consumption by Mankiw (1981), Hansen and
Singleton (1981) and Hall (1982), we attempt to estimate directly the
form of U in (3) without specifying a model capable of predicting the
chosen levels of C_t and L_t. We exploit the restrictions on the data
imposed by the first-order conditions necessary for the maximization of
(3) subject to a budget constraint.

We assume the representative individual has access to some financial
assets which can be both bought and sold. In addition, he has access
spot markets in which labor and consumption are freely traded. As long
as the optimum path lies in the interior of the budget set, we can use
simple perturbation arguments to establish certain characteristics of
this optimal path. At any point along an optimal path, the
representative individual cannot make himself better off by foregoing one
unit of consumption or leisure at time t and using the proceeds to
purchase any other good at any other point in time. In particular, when
the representative individual is following his optimal path of
consumption and leisure, these three first order conditions must hold.

$$(S) \quad \frac{\partial U / \partial C_t}{\partial U / \partial L_t} = \frac{P_t}{W_t}$$

$$(EC): \quad E_t \frac{\rho \partial U / \partial C_{t+1}}{\partial U / \partial C_t} \cdot \frac{P_t (1 + r_t)}{P_{t+1}} - 1 = 0$$

$$(EL): \quad E_t \; \rho \; \frac{\partial U/\partial \; L_{t+1}}{\partial U/\partial L_t} \; \frac{W_t(1+r_t)}{W_{t+1}} \; - 1 = 0$$

Here, P_t is the nominal price of a unit of C_t, W_t is the wage the individual receives when he foregoes one unit of L_t and r_t is the nominal return from holding a security between t and t+1.[2]

The static first-order condition (S) says that the individual cannot make himself better off by foregoing one unit of consumption (thereby decreasing his utility by $\partial U/\partial C_t$) and spending the proceeds (P_t) on P_t/W_t units of leisure each of which he values at $\partial U/\partial L_t$. The reverse transaction is also unable to increase his utility. Note that the model implies that equation (S) holds exactly. Since we assume at time t the consumer knows the real wage $\left(\frac{W}{P}\right)_t$, he choses consumption and leisure to equate the real wage and the marginal rate of substitution.

The Euler equation for consumption (EC) states that along an optimal path the representative individual cannot alter his expected utility by giving up one unit of consumption in period t, investing its cost in any available security, and consuming the proceeds in period t+1. The utility cost of giving up a unit of consumption in period t is given by $\partial U/\partial C_t$. The expected utility gain is given by $E_t \rho \partial U/\partial C_{t+1} \cdot \frac{P_t}{P_{t+1}}(1 + r_t)$. Equating the cost and gain from this perturbation yields the first-order condition (EC). It is important to be clear about the generality of this result. The condition (EC) will hold even if labor supply cannot be

---

[2] If more than one security is available, (EC) and (EL) should hold for all securities which can be freely bought and sold.

freely chosen, and trading is not possible in many assets, as long as some asset exists which is either held in positive amounts or for which borrowing is possible.

Finally, the Euler equation for leisure (EL) asserts that along an optimal path the representative individual cannot improve his welfare by working one hour more at t, (thereby losing $\partial U/\partial L_t$ of utility) and using his earnings W_t to purchase a security whose proceeds will be used to buy back $\dfrac{W_t(1+r_t)}{W_{t+1}}$ of leisure at t+1 in all states of nature. Such an investment would increase expected utility by $E_t \rho [\partial U/\partial L_{t+1}]\, W_t(1+r_t)/W_{t+1}$. Therefore (EL) ensures that this expression is equal to $\partial U/\partial L_t$.

If the static first order condition (S) held exactly one of (EC) and (EL) would be redundant. We can see this by replacing $\partial U/\partial C_t$ and $\partial U/\partial C_{t+1}$ in (EC) using (S). This procedure produces (EL). However, since (S) is unlikely to hold exactly in the data we use the information in all three of these first-order conditions to estimate the parameters of the utility function (1).[3]

---

[3]Even if (S) doesn't hold exactly, the residual in one of the Euler equations is equal to the residual in the other Euler equation times a deterministic function of the residual of (S) at t divided by a deterministic function of the residual of S at t+1. The fact that there is no linear relationship between the three residuals suggests, as will be argued below, that the three equations should be estimated simultaneously.

In order to estimate the instantaneous utility function U, it is necessary to specify a functional form. The most general utility function we use is:

$$U(C_t, L_t) = \frac{1}{1-\gamma} \left[\frac{C_t^{1-\alpha} - 1}{1 - \alpha} + d \frac{L_t^{1-\beta} - 1}{1 - \beta} \right]^{1-\gamma}. \tag{4}$$

This utility function which is similar to MaCurdy's (1981) has, as special cases, an additively separable utility function in consumption and leisure, $(\gamma=0)$;[4] a CES form for the ordinal utility function characteristizing single period decision making, $(\alpha=\beta)$;[5] and a logarithmic utility function, $(\alpha=1, \beta=1, \gamma=0)$. This functional form also provides for the possibility of differential degrees of intertemporal substitution in consumption and leisure. This is easiest to see when $\gamma=0$, so that $\frac{1}{\alpha}$ represents the elasticity of intertemporal substitution of

---

[4] This is the utility function considered by Altonji (1981) and Blinder (1978) among others.

[5] In fact we consider a slight variation of (4) when we impose $\alpha=\beta$. This variation which has been used by Auerbach and Kotlikoff (1981) and Lipton and Sachs (1981) is given by: $\left[C_t^{1-\alpha} + d L_t^{1-\alpha} \right]^{\frac{1-\gamma}{1-\alpha}}$. This utility function has the advantage that α and γ are readily interpretable. $1/\alpha$ is the elasticity of substitution of consumption for leisure while $1/\gamma$ is the intertemporal elasticity of substitution of the composite good $\left[C_t^{1-\alpha} + d \ell_t^{1-\alpha} \right]^{\frac{1}{1-\alpha}}$.

consumption and $\frac{1}{\beta}$ represents the corresponding elasticity for leisure.[6]

Previous work on intertemporal substitution in consumption estimates the condition (EC) maintaining the hypothesis that $\gamma=0$. Even if this supposition is correct, it is clear that this is not an efficient estimation procedure since it neglects the information contained in (S). Given the failures of overidentifying restrictions in the previous research, it seems worthwhile to entertain the hypothesis that the marginal utility of consumption depends also on the level of leisure enjoyed by consumers.

Below we describe how to statistically test the orthogonality restrictions implied by the hypothesis of dynamic optimization. Here it is useful to describe how the parameter estimates can be used to examine the issues of economic interest. An argument can be made that this provides a more satisfactory way of testing the relevance of the model than is provided by statistical tests of overidentifying restrictions. The model is at best an approximation to reality. Therefore, with enough data the point hypotheses corresponding to the overidentifying restrictions will be rejected at any given critical value. On this view, testing these hypotheses sheds as much light on the quantity of data available as on the model's validity as an approximation of reality. The last question can only be answered by estimating parameters which correspond to magnitudes relevant for assessing the reasonableness of the theory. In any event, this methodological issue is moot in the context

---

[6]This elasticity is simply the percentage change in the ratio of consumption (or leisure) at t+1 to consumption (or leisure) at t over the percentage change in the real interest rate $P_t(1+r_t)/P_{t+1}$ (or $W_t(1+r_t)/W_{t+1}$). Elasticities like these have been studied by Hall (1981) and Hansen and Singleton (1981).

of this paper, since both the statistical tests of the model and the parameter estimates point to a common conclusion.

We assess the estimates in two ways: by checking that they obey the restrictions on utility functions implied by economic theory, and more importantly by examining the implied values of short and long run elasticities. Theory requires that the function U be concave; otherwise, the first-order conditions corresponds to a local minimum or saddle point rather than a local maximum. We check this by verifying that the matrix of second derivatives of U is negative definite at all points in our sample.

In informal discussion of the importance of intertemporal substitution, it is often pointed out that the responses of consumption and leisure to temporary changes in prices and wages must be different from the response to permanent changes in these magnitudes. However, the actual responses are impossible to compute without first solving the stochastic control problem whose objection is (3). Instead, we compute some simple measure of responses of consumption and leisure. We derive all measures under the assumption that individuals face a deterministic environment.

The "short-run" elasticities illustrate the changes in consumption and leisure at t in response to temporary changes in W_t, P_t and r_t. We derive these elasticities under the assumption that the effects of these changes on consumption and leisure after t can be neglected. These effects are all mediated through the change in total wealth at t+1 that results from the changes in W_t, P_t and r_t. Insofar as this change in wealth must be very small compared to the wealth of the individual at $t+1$ if he still has long to live, this approximation is valid. The "short-run" elasticities can be computed by totally differentiating (EC) and (EL):

$$
\begin{bmatrix}
C_t \partial^2 U/\partial C_t^2 & L_t \partial^2 U/\partial C_t \partial L_t \\
C_t \partial^2 U/\partial C_t \partial L_t & L_t \partial^2 U/\partial L_t^2 \\
P_t \dfrac{(1+r_t)}{P_{t+1}} \rho \partial U/\partial C_{t+1} & 0 \\
0 & \dfrac{W_t(1+r_t)}{W_{t+1}} \rho \partial U/\partial L_{t+1}
\end{bmatrix}
\begin{bmatrix}
dC_t/C_t \\
dL_t/L_t
\end{bmatrix}
$$

$$
\begin{bmatrix}
(1+^r_t)\dfrac{P_t}{P_{t+1}} \rho \partial U/\partial C_{t+1} \\
\dfrac{(1+r_t)W_t}{W_{t+1}} \rho \partial U/\partial L_{t+1}
\end{bmatrix}
\begin{bmatrix}
dP_t/P_t \\
dW_t/W_t \\
dr_t/1+r_t
\end{bmatrix}
\qquad (5)
$$

If one were interested in the long-run effects of a change in the income tax on consumption and hours worked, the elasticities in (5) would not be very informative. Instead, one would be interested in a measure of the extent to which consumption and labor supply is affected on average over the individual's lifetime. One simple measure of this long-run response is obtained from assuming that the individual has no nonlabor income, that both the real interest rate in terms of leisure and the one in terms of consumption $(\dfrac{P_t(1+r_t)}{P_{t+1}}$ and $\dfrac{W_t(1+r_t)}{W_{t+1}})$ are equal to $1/\rho$ and that the real wage is constant. Then, the individual plans to

maintain a constant level of consumption and of leisure over his
lifetime. His plan is consistent with a static budget constraint which
makes his expenditure on consumption equal to his labor income:

$$C_t - \frac{W_t}{P_t}(N - L_t) = 0 \tag{6}$$

where N is his endowment of leisure. Totally differentiating (6) and (S)
one obtains the following long-run elasticities:

$$
\begin{bmatrix}
C_t & \dfrac{W}{P}L_t \\[2ex]
\dfrac{C_t \partial^2 U/\partial C_t^2}{\partial U/\partial L_t} \quad \dfrac{C_t \partial U/\partial C_t \partial^2 U/\partial C_t \partial \ell_t}{(\partial U/\partial L_t)^2} & \dfrac{L_t \partial^2 U/\partial C_t \partial L_t}{\partial U/\partial L_t} - \dfrac{L_t \partial U/\partial C_t \partial^2 U/\partial L_t^2}{(\partial U/\partial L_t)^2}
\end{bmatrix}
\begin{bmatrix}
\dfrac{dC_t}{C} \\[2ex]
\dfrac{dL_t}{L_t}
\end{bmatrix}
$$

$$
\begin{bmatrix}
(N - L_t)\dfrac{W_t}{P_t} \\[2ex]
\dfrac{P_t}{W_.}
\end{bmatrix}
\dfrac{d(W_t/P_t)}{(W_t/P_t)} \tag{7}
$$

IV. DATA

Estimation of the parameters of (4) requires several choices about
the data to be used. These choices reflect auxiliary assumptions which
must be made in order to test the hypothesis of market clearing and
dynamic optimization. These auxiliary assumptions are of pivotal

importance because the estimation results depend on their validity as well as on the basic theoretical notions being examined. This subsection describes the assumptions underlying the estimates in the paper.

The first-order conditions (S), (EC), and (EL) characterize optimization for a single individual with a given utility function. Their application to aggregate data is more problematic. Rubinstein (1975) presents results showing that if all individuals have identical, separable utility functions, and if all risky assets including human capital are freely traded, the model we consider here can be rigorously justified as applied to aggregate data. To state these conditions is to recognize their falsity. They imply that the consumption of all individuals should be perfectly correlated. Hall and Mishkin (1981) present data indicating that, at least using one measure of consumption, there is only negligible correlation between the consumption of different individuals.[7] It is standard in studying consumption to model per capita consumption as if it were chosen by a representative consumer. We follow the standard convention of using consumption and labor input per member of the adult population. As Summers (1982) points out, the rationale for this procedure is unclear. If it is appropriate to give individuals under 16 zero weight, presumably because they consume little, might it not also be appropriate to weight individuals of different ages according

---

[7] Grossman and Shiller present another aggregation theorem. However their theorem cannot be used to rigorously justify the estimation of a representative consumer's utility function as is done here. Their results are only local and so do not apply over the discrete intervals which generate the data, unless the utility function has a special form, different from the one assumed here. Furthermore, their theorem assumes interior solutions for each agent, which is unrealistic for leisure.

to their consumption or labor supply in constructing per-capita
variables? This approach is taken in Summers (1982) where it has a
significant impact on the results. It is not pursued here because of the
difficulty in finding a population index which is appropriate for both
consumption and leisure.

The choice of the measure of consumption is fundamental. Here the
distinction between consumption and consumption expenditure is crucial.
Even goods classified as non-durables in the National Income Accounts
have a durable component, as has been pointed out by Mankiw (1982). The
pen with which this sentence is written was purchased nine months ago.
Clothing is another obvious example of a durable good which is officially
classified as a non-durable. Even services are in many ways like durable
goods. Utility comes not from trips to the doctor but from the stream of
good health which they provide. Vacations are taken in part for the
memories they create. Thus all of the available data pertain to
consumption expenditure not actual consumption and so are not strictly
appropriate. We use as our measure of consumption alternatively real
expenditures on non-durables and non-durables and services as reported in
the National Income and Product Accounts. The NIPA price deflators are
used to measure prices.

The choice of a consumption concept poses a second fundamental
issue, that of separability of the utility function. Both measures of
consumption with which we experiment in this study can only proxy part of
total consumption since the expenditure and the services from durable
goods are completely excluded. Implicitly each of our alternative

specifications impose the assumption that the excluded forms of consumption enter the utility function in additively separable ways. This assumption which has been maintained in all the earlier work on consumption is obviously problematic. Consider freezers and food, or cars and gasoline. An alternative defense of using a subset of consumption as a proxy for aggregate consumption is to rely on Hicks or Leontief aggregation.[8] If the relative price of different types of consumption is fixed and the utility function is homothetic, or if different goods are consumed in fixed proportions, any subset of aggregate consumption can be used as a proxy for total consumption. The data do not provide much support for either of these assumptions.

The measurement of leisure also poses problems. Somewhat arbitrarily we specify that the representative individual has a time endowment of $7 \times 16 = 112$ hours a week. We compute leisure by subtracting per-capita total hours worked by the civilian labor force from this time endowment. In principle, it would be possible to estimate econometrically the size of the time endowment. In practice, this parameter is difficult to estimate so we constrain it a priori. The specification we adopt here based on total hours worked is open to the serious criticism that it does not distinguish between changes in the number of persons working and in average hours per worker. The former poses serious problems for the model since the first-order conditions (S)

---

[8] If reliance is placed on Leontief aggregation, there is still a problem of measuring real returns, unless a price index for all consumption is employed.

and (EL) need not hold for individuals whose labor supply is at the corner solution of zero hours worked.

The measurement of the price of leisure, the wage, also involves a choice between less than fully satisfactory alternatives. The series we use refers to average total compensation of employees in the non-farm business sector. We calculate after tax wages by using a time series of marginal tax rates on labor income, measured as the sum of Federal Income taxes,[9] Social Security taxes and state income taxes. The problems with this measure of wages include its partial coverage, and its failure to include some forms of compensation such as the accrual of Social Security and private pension benefits. Perhaps more seriously, the extent to which market wages reflect the marginal return from working has been seriously questioned. Hall (1980) argues that certain features of the economy's cyclical behavior can be explained by assuming wages do not reflect true compensation for working on a period by period basis, even though the economy always attains the Walrasian equilibrium level of employment.

The final data decision is the choice of an asset return r. We experimente with both estimates of the before and after tax Treasury Bill interest rate. As a crude approximation, we assume a 30 percent tax rate on interest income. Since the results are fairly similar, only the after tax results are reported. This choice is appropriate for recent years when savings instruments paying near market rates of return were widely

---

[9] The data on average Federal marginal tax rates came from Seatar (1981).

available. Its appropriateness is less clear during the bulk of the
sample period when interest rate ceilings constrained the rates
obtainable by most individuals. The extent to which installment credit
rates match with the treasury bill rate is not clear. Summers (1982)
finds very similar results in a study of fluctuations in consumption
which uses both time deposit and treasury bill yields. The time deposit
rate is not used here because data are not available over a large enough
period.

A final issue to be addressed is the appropriate period of
observation. As is by now well known, the use of discrete time data can
lead to biases if the data are generated by a continuous time process.
In particular, time averages of a random walk will not have serially
uncorrelated increments. There is the additional problem that the link
between consumption and consumption expenditure is likely to be better
at lower than at higher frequencies.

Because of the latter problem we reject the common view that models
of this type should be estimated with data for as short of a period as
possible. In addition the assumption of additive separability is more
realistic for large period lengths. We use two different procedures.
The first, which we employ with apology but without excuse, is to use
seasonally adjusted quarterly data. There is clearly a serious risk that
the averaging involved in seasonal adjustment disturbs the results. The
second procedure involves using only data from the fourth quarter of each
year. The interval between observations reduces time aggregation
problems. In addition, the gap between observations may reduce the

problems which come from the use of expenditure to proxy consumption. Finally, the use of data from only one quarter may reduce seasonality problems.

We use three lists of instruments for every specification we estimate. List A includes a constant, the rates of inflation between $t-2$ and $t-1$ and between $t-5$ and $t-1$, the nominal rate of return between $t-1$ and t and the holding period yield between $t-5$ and $t-1$. List B includes a constant and the levels of consumption, the interest rate, leisure, prices and wages at $t-1$ and $t-2$. Instead list C includes the values of these variables at t and $t-1$. Therefore, list C allows us to check whether the estimates worsen when current variables are included as instruments.

V. ESTIMATION METHOD

We estimate the parameters α, β, d and γ of the function U given by (4). This is done by fitting the implied first order conditions (S), (EC) and (EL) to U.S. data. Hansen and Singleton (1981) suggest that the theoretically correct method for estimating Euler Equations like (EC) and (EL) is a nonlinear instrumental variables procedure. The rationale for this procedure can be stated as follows: The equations (EC) and (EL) state that the expectation at t of a function of variables at t and $(t+1)$ is zero. Hence they can be written as $E_t h(X_{t+1}, \theta) = 0$, where h is a vector function, X_{t+1} includes variables at t and $t+1$ and θ is a vector of parameters. However, this states that the expectation of the product of any variable in the information set at t with the actual values of $h(X_{t+1}, \theta)$ must be zero. This suggests as a natural estimator for θ the value of θ which minimizes an appropriately weighted sum of the squares of the product of instruments at t with $h(X_{t+1}, \theta)$. In particular, Hansen and Singleton (1981) propose that the value of θ be chosen which minimizes:

$$J = h' \ Z \ H \ Z' \ h \qquad (8))$$

where h is the qT x 1 vector of actual values of $h(X_{t+1}, \theta)$, q is the number of equations, T the number of observations, H is a weighting matrix while Z is the qT x mq matrix given by:

$$
Z = \begin{vmatrix}
Z & 0 & 0 & \cdots \\
0 & Z & 0 & \\
0 & & & \\
\cdot & & &
\end{vmatrix}
$$

where there are as many blocks of Z as there are equations and Z is the T x m matrix of observations on instruments.[10]   Here, m is the number of instruments. Hansen and Singleton (1981) derive the weighting matrix which produces the smallest assymptotic standard errors for θ even when

---

[10]Note that the product of the instruments and the residual of (EL) at t is not a linear function or products of the instruments with the residuals of the other two equations. Therefore, if only two equations were estimated the results would depend on which two were chosen. Therefore, we have chosen instead to estimate all three equations at once with a common set of instruments.

the h's are heteroskedastic conditional on the Z's as long as they are
not unconditionally heteroskedastic. For simplicity, we assume instead
that the h's are also conditionally homoskedastic. This leads to
consistent estimates although the standard errors are inconsistent if the
assumption of homoskedasticity is wrong. In the case we consider, the
"optimal" H reduces to the familiar three stage least squares formula:

$$H = \left[\ \hat{S}^{-1} \otimes (Z'Z)^{1}\ \right]$$

where S is the covariance matrix of the h's of different equations. Here
the h's are the fitted values of h after a two stage least squares
estimation procedure which minimizes (8) using $I \otimes (Z'Z)^{1}$ as the
weighting matrix.

Hansen (1981) also shows that the minimized value of J when the
"optimal" H is used is assymptotically distributed as χ^2 with degrees of
freedom equal to (qm − r) where r is the number of parameters that are
estimated. This provides a very simple test of the overidentifying
restrictions.[11] These restrictions simply require that the addition of
extra instruments shouldn't increase the value of J very much. This is
so because, according to the model, at the true θ, the expectation of the
cross product of any new instrument and h is zero.

---

[11]Hansen's theorem strictly applies only to situations in which the
variables are stationary and ergodic. This requirement is probably met
by our first list or instruments while it is less likely to old for lists
B and C.

The main problem with using any variable in the information set at t as an instrument is that this procedure is appropriate only when the sole reason for h to differ from zero is that, at t+1, agents discover new information about prices and incomes. If this were indeed the only source of uncertainty in the economy then the static condition (S) would hold exactly; there is no reason for the marginal rate of substitution of consumption for leisure to be different from the real wage. However, it is inevitable that any empirical estimate of (S) will not fit perfectly. Any of the natural explanations or this residual seem to invalidate the use as instruments of all the variables known at t. Such explanations include the presence of errors of measurement of the variables, errors of specification, the presence of nominal contracts and the absence of full information by the agents at t about variables which occur at t. These last two explanations for the residual in (S) appear to be consistent with assuming that all three first order conditions hold in expectation with respect to a weaker conditioning set than the one Hansen and Singleton (1981) suggest.

In particular, in a model like that of Fischer (1977) these conditions might hold for every agent when the expectation is taken conditional on the variables known when the nominal contract which prevails at t is signed. Likewise, in a model like that of Lucas (1973) they would hold when the conditioning set is the set of economy wide variables known by agents at t. However, the aggregation over agents who signed contracts at different dates or over agents who have different private information might present serious difficulties. In any event, these considerations suggest that an appropriate estimator of α, β, d and γ can be obtained by estimating the system of equations (S), (EL) and (EC) by nonlinear three stage least squares where the instruments are variables whose realizations occur before t. In fact, we compare the results of using current and lagged instruments with those of using only lagged instruments.

VI. RESULTS

We begin by estimating the three first-order conditions separately, since each of these equations requires a different set of assumptions regarding which markets clear. We then estimate the entire system of equations. These system estimates require that the individual does not face a quantity constraint in any market. Because our preliminary results using only fourth quarter data are essentially identical to those using quarterly data, we report only the latter.

The first Euler equation (EC) requires that the expectation of the product of the marginal rate of substitution between consumption in t and consumption in t+1 with the real interest rate equals unity. This condition holds so long as the individual is not constrained either in the goods market or in the capital market. In particular, (EC) does not embody any assumption regarding the determination of the level of employment.

Table 1 contains the estimates of (EC) imposing additive separability between consumption and leisure ($\gamma=0$) as is done implicitly

Table 1

Estimates of Euler Equation for Consumption (EC) Separable Case

	(1)	(2)	(3)	(4)	(5)	(6)
Consumption measure	ND	ND	ND	ND+S	ND+S	ND+S
Instrument List	A	B	C	A	B	C
α	.234	.174	.512	.330	.092	.333
	(.219)	(.199)	(.193)	(.237)	(.209)	(.182)
ρ [1]	.997	.997	.996	.996	.997	.996
	(.001)	(.001)	(.001)	(.001)	(.001)	(.001)
Concave?	YES	YES	YES	YES	YES	YES
	25.48	43.06	35.43	24.8	47.41	44.78
Critical J* at 1%	11.34	21.66	21.66	11.34	21.66	21.66

Standard errors are in parentheses.

in earlier work. The estimates of α are positive, as is necessary for concavity. They vary between .09 and .51, and center at about .3. Other studies estimate this Euler equation in the additively separable case and generally report higher estimates of α. Hansen and Singleton (1981) find α to be about .8, Summers (1982) about 3, Mankiw (1981) about 4, and Hall (1981) about 15. In all cases, the overidentifying restrictions are clearly rejected, indicating that the orthogonality conditions upon which these estimates are premised do not hold. This is precisely the same rejection Hansen and Singleton (1981) and Mankiw (1981) report. Beyond the variations in the measure of consumption and the instrument list shown in the table, we also experimented with the use of pre-tax returns, with little impact on the results.

The failure of the overidentifying restrictions suggests that it is likely that parameter estimates will be sensitive to the choice of instruments lists. In a different context, Hausman (1978) shows that the difference between estimates obtained with different instrument lists can be used as a basis for an exogeneity test. If adding instruments changes the results by "too much" the hypothesis that the additional instruments are exogenous can be rejected. We suspect, but have not been able to prove, that the exogeneity tests used here can be given an interpretation as Hausman tests.

Table 2 contains the estimates of (EC) that allow non-separability between consumption and leisure. The standard errors of the parameter estimates are extremely high. In particular, we cannot reject the null hypothesis of additive separability between consumption and leisure ($\gamma=0$). This is not surprising, as the difficulty of testing separability

Table 2

Estimates of Euler Equation for Consumption (EC) Nonseparable Case

	(1)	(2)	(3)	(4)	(5)	(6)
Consumption measure	ND	ND	ND	ND+S	ND+S	ND+S
Instrument List	A	B	C	A	B	C
α	1.118	.257	.375	-.204	.147	.799
	(118.13)	(1.568)	(1.302)	(15.94)	(4.112)	(.393)
β	-45.827	151.9	150.99	-71.39	134.5	-41.858
	(12839.8)	(472.3)	(612.97)	(872.6)	(248.95)	(800.2)
	-4.730	.098	.086	-.537	.1780	.034
	(1299.3)	(1.592)	(1.329)	(21.8)	(3.757)	(.549)
d	1.383	280.8	280.0	301.2	264.3	284.2
	(332.3)	(3480.0)	(3364.8)	(23595.)	(2840)	(4454.)
ρ [1]	.999	.997	.997	1.001	.996	.993
	(.048)	(.001)	(.001)	(.015)	(.002)	(.002)
Concave?	NO	YES	YES	NO	YES	NO
		29.23	24.63		33.51	27.50
Critical J* at 1%		16.81	16.81		16.81	16.81

Standard errors are in parentheses.

restrictions is well known. Alternative values of α, β, and γ have very similar implications for the short-run and long-run behavioral elasticities. For example, if d is close to zero, it will be impossible to separately identify α and γ. Furthermore, we continue to reject the overidentifying restrictions. Thus, the rejection of the model Hansen and Singleton (1981) and Mankiw (1981) report cannot be attributed to their maintained hypothesis of separability between consumption and leisure.

The second Euler equation (EL) specifies that the product of the marginal rate of substitution of leisure in t and leisure in t+1 and the real interest rate in terms of leisure has an expectation of 1. This condition is premised upon the absence of quantity constraints both in the capital market and in the labor market.

Table 3 presents the estimates of (EL) in the additive separable case. The estimates of β often have the wrong sign (negative), rejecting the concavity restriction. Note that when the concavity restriction is violated, the estimated parameters imply a utility function whose maximum is given by a corner solution, or which does not exist. Obviously the data decisively reject either possibility. In principle, concavity of the utility should be imposed, as the likelihood of observed consumption and leisure is zero if the utility function is not concave. In practice, imposing this restriction is difficult. Therefore, it is hard to interpret in a very meaningful way the standard errors or the parameters in the case where the concavity restrictions are rejected. Nonetheless, the data indicates no clear relation between the quantity of leisure and the relative price of present versus future leisure. This result casts

Table 3

Estimates of Euler Equation for Leisure (EL) Separable Case

	(1)	(2)	(3)
Instrument List	A	B	C
β	-.739	-.996	.121
	(.959)	(.474)	(.480)
ρ [1]	.994	.994	.994
	(.001)	(.001)	(.001)
Concave?	NO	NO	YES
	8.47	15.75	21.7
Critical J* at 1%	11.35	21.66	21.66

Standard errors are in parentheses.

Table 4

Estimates of Euler Equation for Leisure (EL) Nonseparable Case

	(1)	(2)	(3)	(4)	(5)	(6)
Consumption measure	ND	ND	ND	ND+S	ND+S	ND+S
Instrument List	A	B	C	A	B	C
α	2.286	-.227	1.6332	1.696	1.970	2.947
	(5.490	(39.4)	(35.9)	(2.975)	(2.434)	(64.315)
β	8.753	-1.032	.1837	13.083	7.23	.481
	(22.78)	(4.504)	(52.0)	(19.374)	(11.49)	(2344.9)
	-18.42	-.318	-.466	-21.457	-18.8	-9.678
	(217.3)	(9.155)	(30.4)	(143.31)	(110.1)	(1754.)
d	.528	1.132	.510	1.355	.478	.021
	(7.763)	(344.3)	(118.7)	(13.5)	(3.305)	(121.9)
ρ [1]	.995	.995	.994	1.0002	.996	.994
	(.001)	(.0001)	(.0009)	(.008)	(.002)	(.002)
Concave?	NO	NO	NO	NO	NO	BARELY[1]
		8.26	21.63		5.76	25.47
Critical J* at 1%		16.81	16.81		16.81	16.81

Standard errors are in parentheses.

[1] The determinant of the matrix of second partials of U is negative, but very close to zero, making inversion of the matrix, and thus computation of elasticities, impossible.

serious doubt on the premise of most classical macro-economic models that observed labor supply represents unconstrained choices given perceived opportunities. Note especially that the results are not very sensitive to the choice of instrument list. In particular, the use of lagged instruments to capture the possibility of imperfect information has little effect on the results.

Table 4 presents the estimates of (EL) that allow non-separability. The standard errors are huge, and thus do not reject separability. The estimated utility function is almost never concave. Hence, the failure reported above for the separable case cannot be attributed to the then maintained hypothesis of separability.

The third condition (S), which equates the marginal rate of substitution between consumption and leisure to the real wage, is the crucial test of labor-market-clearing. Unlike either of the other first-order conditions, this static relation does not rely upon the assumed absence of liquidity-constraints. It relies only upon the ability of the individual to trade-off consumption and leisure within a single period. In other words, it assumes only that there is no quantity constraint either in the goods market or in the labor market. Since consumers are generally not constrained in the goods market, this equation should hold so long as observed employment lies on the labor supply curve. Recall that the underlying model also predicts that (S) should hold exactly.

Table 5 presents the estimates obtained from the estimation of (S), which has the same form for both the separable and nonseparable utility

Table 5

Estimates of Static Condition (S)

	(1)	(2)	(3)	(4)	(5)	(6)
Consumption measure	ND	ND	ND	ND+S	ND+S	ND+S
Instrument List	A	B	C	A	B	C
α	1.873	2.377	4.636	3.694	3.639	2.789
	(.118)	(.053)	(.040)	(.035)	(.032)	(.032)
β	.018	-1.107	-8.042	-5.426	-16.231	-.212
	(1.417)	(1.097)	(5.306)	(10.038)	(9.324)	(4.235)
	63.98	118.05	118.97	87.91	118.25	121.86
Critical J* at 1%	9.21	20.09	20.09	9.21	20.09	20.09

Standard errors are in parentheses.

functions. In almost every case, the estimate of α is positive, and the estimate of β is negative. We find these signs for different instrument lists, for different measures of consumption, for different frequency data, and for different estimation periods. Although not displayed, these signs also emerge when (S) is estimated in first differences. Altonji (1981) also estimates a version of (S) and reports estimates of α and β with these signs. The data inescapably point to at least one robust result. For any given real wage, consumption and leisure move in opposite directions in response to other exogenous changes.

This result provides powerful evidence against the hypothesis that observed labor supply behavior can be described as resulting from continuous maximization of a stable additively separable intertemporal utility function. The estimated utility function is extremely implausible, as can be illustrated easily. Holding the real wage constant, consider an increase in non-labor income. If α and β have opposite signs, then either consumption or leisure must fall. That is, since consumption and leisure move in opposite directions for any given real wage, one must be inferior if the movements represent voluntary maximizing behavior.

These results are due to the fact that over the business cycle consumption and leisure move in opposite directions. At the same time, we simply do not observe at the aggregate level the procyclical movements in the real wage which would make this behavior rational for households.

We next estimate the three first-order conditions jointly as a system. For (EC), (EL) and (S) all to hold, the representative

Table 6

System Estimates

Separable Case

	(1)	(2)	(3)	(4)	(5)	(6)
ion re	ND	ND	ND	ND+S	ND+S	ND+S
nt List	A	B	C	A	B	C
	1.45	1.535	1.570	.793	.889	.904
	(.038)	(.025)	(.026)	(.017)	(.015)	(.016)
	-1.181	-.704	-.236	-3.030	-1.366	-1.100
	(.799)	(.389)	(.407)	(.470)	(.284)	(.290)
	.994	.994	.994	.994	.993	.993
	(.001)	(.001)	(.001)	(.001)	(.0004)	(.0004)
	NO	NO	NO	NO	NO	NO
	30.67	55.23	56.51	50.75	109.76	125.09
J^*	24.73	49.59	49.59	24.73	49.59	49.59

Standard errors are in parentheses.

Table 7
System Estimates
Non-Separable Case

	(1)	(2)	(3)	(4)	(5)	(6)
Consumption measure	ND	ND	ND	ND+S	ND+S	ND+S
Instrument List	A	B	C	A	B	C
α	1.407	1.680	1.713	.789	.889	.928
	(.030)	(.033)	(.035)	(.017)	(.014)	(.018)
β	-4.937	-.340	.158	-3.637	-1.718	-.688
	(.549)	(.414)	(.493)	(.464)	(.281)	(.324)
	-6.452	.050	.321	-2.720	-2.716	.080
	(1.791)	(.035)	(1.178)	(.967)	(.602)	(.176)
d	.843	146.406	16.540	8.297	-.640	114.612
	(.448)	(71.198)	(68.970)	(4.112)	(.776)	(310.028)
ρ [1]	.997	.994	.993	.999	.997	.993
	(.001)	(.0005)	(.001)	(.001)	(.001)	(.0005)
Concave?	NO	YES	YES	NO	NO	YES
J	21.308	41.91	47.23	31.45	99.07	128.24
Critical J* at 1%	21.67	46.96	46.96	21.67	46.96	46.96

Standard errors are in parentheses.

Table 8

System Estimates Imposing $\alpha = \beta$

Separable Case

	(1)	(2)	(3)	(4)	(5)	(6)
Consumption measure	ND	ND	ND	ND+S	ND+S	ND+S
Instrument List	A	B	C	A	B	C
α	1.506	1.554	1.608	.948	1.005	1.012
	(.030)	(.022)	(.028)	(.019)	(.019)	(.019)
ρ 1	.993	.993	.993	.993	.993	.993
	(.001)	(.001)	(.001)	(.001)	(.001)	(.001)
Concave?	YES	YES	YES	YES	YES	YES
	38.21	66.82	59.44	61.65	119.06	117.81
Critical J* at 1%	26.22	50.89	50.89	26.22	50.89	50.89

Standard errors are in parentheses.

Table 9

System Estimates Imposing $\alpha = \beta$

Non-Separable Case

	(1)	(2)	(3)	(4)	(5)	(6)
Consumption measure	ND	ND	ND	ND+S	ND+S	ND+S
Instrument List	A	B	C	A	B	C
α	1.635	1.600	1.648	1.722	1.079	1.019
	(.112)	(.023)	(.023)	(.040)	(.026)	(.027)
	-3.486	-.563	1.068	-7.757	-1.092	.892
	(2.246)	(.557)	(.599)	(5.554)	(.776)	(.639)
d	.730	.447	.112	.226	.403	-.613
	(.381)	(.115)	(.209)	(.100)	(.242)	(1.496)
ρ [1]	.996	.995	.994	1.002	.999	.995
	(.001)	(.0001)	(.001)	(.005)	(.001)	(.001)
Concave?	NO	NO	YES	NO	NO	NO
J	18.80	53.83	63.26	53.38	151.35	110.53
Critical J* at 1%	23.21	48.28	48.28	23.21	48.28	48.28

Standard errors are in parentheses.

individual must face no quantity constraint in any market.

Table 6 presents the system estimates in the separable case. For both consumption measures and for all instrument lists, the estimate of α is positive and the estimate of β is negative. Thus, the estimated utility function is not concave. The data is not consistent with continous dynamic maximization of a utility function that is additively separable in consumption and leisure.

Table 7 presents the system estimates for the non-separable case. The estimated utility function is concave for only half of the estimates. In most of the concave cases, α and β have opposite signs, implying that either consumption or leisure is an inferior good. In addition, we reject the overidentifying restrictions for all concave estimates. Thus, the data does not readily produce reasonable parameter estimates of the representative individual's utility function. This result provides little support to business cycle models that posit continuous dynamic maximization and the absence of quantity constraints.

We next estimate the system imposing the constraint $\alpha=\beta$. The separable estimates are in Table 8. The estimate of α is consistent across instrument lists: 1.5 for nondurables, and 1.0 for nondurables and services. The overidentifying restrictions are always rejected. The nonseparable estimates are in Table 9. The estimated utility function is usually not concave. The overidentifying restrictions almost always can be rejected, while the null hypothesis of separability cannot be rejected.

Various elasticities are presented in Table 10 for those

nonseparable estimates that imply a concave utility function.[8] Since the
estimates of the utility function parameters vary greatly, the estimated
elasticities also vary greatly. The long-run elasticity of consumption
with respect to the wage is approximately .6, and the long-run elasticity
of leisure with respect to the wage is .26, implying a backward-bending
long-run labor supply curve.

[8]These elasticities are computed using data corresponding to the
first quarter of 1980. A problem arises from the fact that all three
equations have a residual in this period. This residual is ignored in
our calculations which use the actual values for C, L, P, W and r on both
sides of (5) and (7). Alternatively, we could have changed some of these
variables to make (S), (EC) and (EL) hold exactly and then computed the
elasticities.

Table 10

Elasticities Implied by the Estimates

Table and Column of Estimates	2.2	2.3	2.5	7.2	7.3	7.€
Short-Run Elasticities						
C with respect to P	-3.1	-2.4	-3.4	-.61	-.60	-1.
C with respect to W	.0055	.0047	.0061	-.64	.55	1.
C with respect to 1+r	-3.1	-2.3	-3.4	-.045	-.045	.
L with respect to P	.0015	.00086	;0038	.0005	-.18	.
L with respect to W	-.0027	-.0028	-.0035	-.36	-.25	.
L with respect to 1+r	-.0013	-.0020	-.00030	-.36	-.22	.
Long-Run Elasticities						
C with respect to W/P					.54	.6
L with respect to W/P					.26	.2

Probably the most important elasticity for evaluating the intertemporal substitution hypothesis is the short-run elasticity of leisure with respect to the current wage. This elasticity varies from -.0027 to -4.2 across estimates. This implies a short-run labor supply elasticity between .01 and 17, since leisure is roughly four times labor supply. Note that the elasticity of leisure with respect to changes in the interest rate is in all cases but one essentially identical to the elasticity with respect to the wage. Hence it too fluctuates widely over different estimates. Moreover, the short run elasticity of consumption with respect to changes in prices varies from -.6 to -3.4. It is not surprising, given the reluctance of the data to be characerized by the three first-order conditions, that these short-run elasticities are not well pinned down.

VII. Conclusions

The empirical results reported in this paper are consistently disappointing. The overidentifying restrictions implied by the model of dynamic optimization in the absence of quantity constraints are rejected by virtually all of the estimates. The estimated utility function parameters always imply implausible behavior. We can conclude that the data strongly reject specifications of the type used in this paper. In this final section, we examine a number of alternative explanations for the results obtained. The abundance of plausible explanations for the results we obtained (or for other results that might have been obtained) leads us to be somewhat skeptical of the power of aggregate time series data in distinguishing alternative macroeconomic hypotheses.

A first possibility is that our poor results are a consequence of problems of measurement and estimation. As emphasized in the initial discussion of the data, our measures of consumption and leisure are all open to question, as is our proxy for real returns. Probably more serious is the use of seasonally adjusted data. Seasonal fluctuations, which account for most of the variance in leisure, should be explained by dynamic optimization rather than averaged out as in our data. Utility presumably depends on actual consumption not on consumption as adjusted by X-11. Time aggregation issues are possibly serious as well.

A second, more likely possibility is that the auxiliary assumptions we maintain to make the problem tractable are false. Aggregation in models of this type is very problematic. It is also possible that our assumption of additive separability across time is the root of the problem. Over some intervals, this assumption is unwarranted. People who have worked hard want to rest. Mealtimes are not staggered through the day by accident. How serious these types of effects are at the macro level remains an open question. Clark and Summers (1979) examine several types of evidence bearing on the effects of previous employment experience on subsequent experience, and conclude that habit formation, and persistence effects predominate over intertemporal substitution effects. This suggests that while non-separability may help to explain the failure of our results, the sign of the key cross derivatives may well be the opposite of that usually assumed in intertemporal substitution theories. Note that this problem of non-separable utility in consumption relates closely to the issues connected with distinguishing between consumption and consumption expenditure.

A third general class of explanation for the results we obtained involves changing tastes. Just as the identification of traditional demand curves depends on the predominance of technological shocks relative to taste shocks, identification in models of the type estimated here depends on the maintained hypothesis of constant tastes. This is clearly a fiction. In every arena where taste shocks are easy to disentangle, fashion being an obvious example, they are pervasive. Even if the tastes of individuals were stable over time, the tastes of individuals of different ages differ, and the age distribution represented by the representative consumer has changed through time. An important topic for future research is the estimation of models which allow for changing tastes, either through random shocks, or endogenously on the basis of experience. The latter possibility relates closely to the problem of non-separability in the utility function.

A final possible reason for the failure of the model is that the assumption that individuals are unconstrained in the labor and capital markets is false. While fully satisfactory theories of wage rigidity have not been developed, the observed data suggest that wages are in fact rigid. The apparently large effects of sharp nominal contractions that have been observed in repeated historic episodes support this view.

Analyses of the macro character of unemployment, such as Clark and

Summers (1979) and Akerlof and Main (1981), find that it is extremely

concentrated among relatively few individuals whose employment is

strongly pro-cyclical. This tends to suggest a role for disequilibrium

in certain labor market segments in explaining cyclical fluctuations.

In sum, the results of this investigation are discouraging. We find

little evidence in favor of any of the models estimated here. In

particular, we conclude that taking account of leisure does not

rationalize the failure of previous models of consumption based on

intertemporal decision making.

Bibliography

Akerlof, George and Brian G.M. Main, "An Experience Weighted Measure of Employment Durations". AER, Dec. 1981, pp. 1003-1011.

Altonji, Joseph G., "Does the Labor Market Clear? A Test Under Alternative Expectations Assumptions". Mimeo, 1980.

Altonji, Joseph G., "The Intertemporal Substitution Model of Labor Market Fluctuations: An Empirical Analysis:. Mimeo, 1981.

Auerbach, Alan S. and Lawrence Kotlikoff, "The Efficiency Gains from Dynamic Tax Return".

Barro, Robert J., "A Capital Market in an Equilibrium Business Cycle Model", Econometrica 48, 1393-1417. September 1980.

Blinder, Alan S., Toward an Economic Theory of Income Distribution, MIT Press, 1974.

Clark, Kim B. and Lawrence H. Summers, "Labor Market Dynamics and Unemployment: A Reconsideration". Brookings Papers on Economic Activity 1: 1979, pp. 13-60.

Clark, Kim B. and Lawrence H. Summers, "Labor Force Participation: Timing and Persistence". Mimeo, 1981.

Fischer, Stanley, "Long Term Contracts, Rational Expectations and the Optimal Money Supply Rule". Journal of Political Economy 85, pp. 191-205, February 1977.

Friedman, Benjamin, Comment on "After Keynesian Macroeconomics" by Robert E. Lucas, Jr. and Thomas Sargent in: After the Phillips Curve: Persistence of High Inflation and High Unemployment, Federal Reserve Bank of Boston, (1978).

Grossman, Sanford and Robert Shiller, "The Determinants of the Variability of Stock Market Prices". American Economic Review Papers and Proceedings, May 1981.

Hall, Robert E., "Stochastic Implications of the Life-Cycle Permanent Income Hypothesis: Theory and Evidence". Journal of Political Economy, 86(6), pp. 971-89, December 1978.

Hall, Robert E., "Employment Fluctuations and Wage Rigidity". Brookings Papers on Economic Activity 1: 1980.

Hall, Robert E., "Labor Supply and Aggregate Fluctuations" in K. Brunner and A. Melger eds., On the State of Macroeconomics. Carnegie-Rochester Conference on Public Policy vol 12, North Holland, Amsterdam, 1980.

Hall, Robert E., "Intertemporal Substitution in Consumption". Mimeo, July 1981.

Hansen, Lars Peter, "Large Sample Properties of Method of Moments Estimators". Mimeo, 1981.

Hansen, Lars Peter and Kenneth Singleton, "Generalized Instrumental Variables Estimation of Nonlinear Rational Expectations Models". Mimeo, 1981, forthcoming in Econometrica.

King, Robert G. and Charles I. Flosser, "The Behavior of Money Credit and Prices in a Real Business Cycle". Mimeo, September 1981.

Kydland, Finn and Edward Prescott, "Time to Build and the Persistence of Unemployment". Mimeo, 1981.

Lipton, David and Jeffrey Sachs, "Accumulation and Growth in a Two Country Model: A Simulation Approach".

Long, John and Charles Flosser, "Real Business Cycles". Mimeo, November 1980.

Lucas, Robert E., Jr., "Some International Evidence on Output-Inflation Tradeoffs". American Economic Review 63, 326-334, June 1973.

Lucas, Robert E., Jr. and Leonard Rapping, "Real Wages, Employment and Inflation". Journal of Political Economy 77, 721-54, September/October 1969.

MaCurdy, Thomas E., "An Empirical Model of Labor Supply in a Life Cycle Setting". Journal of Political Economy 89, 1059-85, December 1981.

MaCurdy, Thomas E., "An Intertemporal Analysis of Taxation and Work Disincentives: An Analysis of the Denver Income Maintenance Experiment". Mimeo, 1981.

Mankiw, N. Gregory, "The Permanent Income Hypothesis and the Real Interest Rate". Economics Letters 7, 307-311 (1981).

Mankiw, N. Gregory, "Hall's Consumption Hypothesis and Durable Goods". Journal of Monetary Economics, forthcoming 1982.

Prescott, Edward C. and Rajnish Mehra, "Recursive Competitive
    Equilibrium: The Case of Homogeneous Households". Econometrica
    48(6), 1365-80, September 1980.

Rubinstein, Mark, "An Aggregation Theorem for Securities Markets".
    Journal of Financial Economics 1, 255-44 (1974).

Seater, John, "Marginal Federal Personal and Corporate Income Tax Rates
    in the U.S. 1909-1975". Research papers of the Philadelphia Federal
    Reserve Bank 57, November 1980.

Summers, Lawrence H., "Tax Policy, The Rate of Return and Savings".
    Mimeo, 1982.

DATA APPENDIX

Per Capita Consumption of Nondurable Goods

1947	1	15.1181	15.3253	15.3145	15.0508
1948	1	14.9965	15.1193	14.9251	15.1231
1949	1	15.176	15.1679	15.0105	15.1684
1950	1	15.2864	15.397	15.6202	15.3359
1951	1	15.7318	15.5684	15.8787	16.01
1952		15.8778	16.218	16.4036	16.5468
1953		16.5085	16.5194	16.3525	16.2695
1954		16.2964	16.1772	16.3403	16.5462
1955		16.6223	16.835	16.9179	17.2254
1956		17.342	17.2493	17.2076	17.2753
1957	1	17.2842	17.3054	17.4953	17.3392
1958		17.0793	17.1669	17.4182	17.5529
1959		17.7135	17.7698	17.7844	17.8401
1960		17.7538	17.9004	17.7241	17.6619
1961		17.7245	17.8361	17.7898	18.0217
1962		18.1356	18.144	18.2191	18.241
1963	1	18.2095	18.2046	18.2686	18.1997
1964	1	18.4467	18.6952	18.9275	18.8923
1965		19.0122	19.0697	19.2591	19.8004
1966	1	19.8806	19.9736	20.0571	19.8963
1967	1	20.0165	20.0267	19.9361	19.9453
1968		20.2717	20.4233	20.6881	20.5674
1969		20.6554	20.6685	20.6322	20.6068
1970		20.6915	20.6665	20.7158	20.7679
1971		20.7305	20.6905	20.5826	20.6065
1972		20.5418	20.9292	21.1102	21.3195
1973	1	21.4016	21.0774	21.0711	20.8738
1974		20.5617	20.4624	20.4872	20.1342
1975		20.2005	20.4478	20.4365	20.4243
1976		20.7229	20.8821	21.0148	21.1827
1977		21.2164	21.2692	21.306	21.6011
1978		21.5059	21.5881	21.8042	22.1046
1979		21.8658	21.7538	21.9646	22.2214
1980	1	22.1486	21.7699	21.5778	21.8319
1981	1	22.0082			

Price Deflator for Nondurable Goods

1947	1	57.3	57.8	58.9	60.8
1948	1	61.7	62.3	62.9	62.2
1949	1	61.3	60.5	59.8	59.5
1950	1	59.2	59.6	61.4	62.7
1951	1	65.3	65.8	65.6	66.4
1952	1	66.5	66.3	66.5	66.8
1953	1	66.4	66.2	66.3	66.3
1954	1	66.6	66.9	66.6	66.4
1955	1	66.4	66.3	66.3	66.2
1956	1	66.4	67.	67.7	68.
1957	1	68.6	69.	69.8	70.
1958	1	71.1	71.2	71.	70.8
1959	1	71.	71.2	71.6	71.9
1960	1	71.8	72.4	72.7	73.3
1961	1	73.4	73.1	73.3	73.3
1962	1	73.6	73.9	74.	74.3
1963	1	74.6	74.6	75.1	75.3
1964	1	75.7	75.7	75.9	76.1
1965	1	76.3	77.2	77.6	78.
1966	1	79.1	79.9	80.4	81.1
1967	1	81.1	81.4	82.2	82.9
1968	1	83.9	84.8	85.6	86.7
1969	1	87.5	88.8	90.	91.3
1970	1	92.5	93.3	93.9	94.9
1971	1	95.2	96.2	97.1	97.9
1972	1	98.8	99.3	100.2	101.6
1973	1	103.7	106.8	109.5	113.1
1974	1	118.1	121.8	124.7	127.9
1975	1	129.2	130.5	133.6	135.1
1976	1	135.5	136.	137.5	138.9
1977	1	141.	142.8	144.1	145.8
1978	1	148.3	152.	154.5	157.9
1979	1	162.9	167.3	172.1	176.9
1980	1	182.9	186.2	190.	195.2
1981	1	199.2			

Per Capita Consumption of Nondurables and Services

Year					
1947	1	27.0029	27.3062	27.1868	26.8148
1948	1	26.9505	27.214	27.0903	27.3367
1949	1	27.3652	27.386	27.1353	27.2766
1950	1	27.5666	28.031	28.3958	28.2527
1951	1	28.7838	28.7001	29.068	29.1406
1952	1	29.1059	29.5682	29.8571	30.1201
1953	1	30.0547	30.1821	30.0416	29.7926
1954	1	29.9176	30.015	30.3785	30.6358
1955	1	30.8897	31.117	31.2747	31.8062
1956		32.0184	32.0416	32.1406	32.3319
1957	1	32.3915	32.4693	32.639	32.5904
1958	1	32.3107	32.6322	33.019	33.133
1959	1	33.5295	33.7377	33.8374	34.076
1960		34.0298	34.3475	34.1464	34.1734
1961	1	34.3721	34.6965	34.6233	35.1102
1962	1	35.3157	35.507	35.6257	35.7823
1963	1	35.7425	35.8456	36.1736	36.2563
1964	1	36.6544	37.0887	37.4717	37.5782
1965	1	37.8054	38.0212	38.3663	39.1592
1966	1	39.3288	39.5447	39.7669	39.7728
1967	1	40.1126	40.2875	40.3474	40.384
1968	1	40.7918	41.2242	41.698	41.7105
1969	1	41.9194	42.0941	42.1803	42.3201
1970	1	42.4848	42.4352	42.6205	42.6579
1971	1	42.7321	42.8002	42.7457	42.951
1972	1	43.0162	43.5023	43.8326	44.3231
1973	1	44.4612	44.2454	44.4331	44.2535
1974		43.8722	43.8509	43.919	43.6346
1975		43.769	44.225	44.2163	44.3262
1976		44.8178	45.0625	45.4028	45.8958
1977		46.0542	46.0632	46.4386	46.9381
1978	1	47.1251	47.4466	47.9977	48.3231
1979		48.3156	48.2977	48.6142	48.9341
1980		48.8883	48.4233	48.5244	48.9224
1981		49.112			

Price Deflator for Nondurables and Services

Year					
1947	1	49.9491	50.4322	51.6095	53.0329
1948	1	53.585	54.1288	54.7721	54.6497
1949	1	54.258	53.9437	53.7245	53.8191
1950	1	53.721	53.8755	55.1427	56.0682
1951	1	57.9071	58.346	58.575	59.4619
1952	1	59.7286	59.9384	60.3772	60.8081
1953	1	60.9484	61.0859	61.5166	61.853
1954		62.186	62.3357	62.2583	62.351
1955	1	62.474	62.5815	62.766	62.9458
1956	1	63.2367	63.722	64.2632	64.6447
1957	1	65.2428	65.6396	66.4104	66.7693
1958	1	67.5642	67.6959	67.8354	67.9774
1959	1	68.1692	68.5026	69.1316	69.5184
1960	1	69.6958	70.1506	70.4884	70.9805
1961	1	71.0762	71.0111	71.3072	71.4017
1962	1	71.7514	72.0895	72.338	72.6342
1963	1	72.9807	73.0737	73.4664	73.7065
1964	1	74.0112	74.1121	74.3656	74.658
1965	1	74.9088	75.5558	76.0066	76.4681
1966		77.2703	78.018	78.6162	79.25
1967	1	79.4972	79.8916	80.5811	81.28
1968	1	82.3401	83.1348	83.887	84.9257
1969	1	85.8765	87.0695	88.2115	89.4009
1970	1	90.5503	91.5047	92.4096	93.6678
1971	1	94.4275	95.5282	96.7369	97.6398
1972	1	98.6432	99.4038	100.355	101.548
1973		103.13	105.333	107.292	109.824
1974	1	113.423	116.413	119.149	121.868
1975	1	123.601	125.069	127.577	129.493
1976	1	130.662	131.868	133.686	135.83
1977	1	138.303	140.539	142.585	144.558
1978	1	146.832	150.147	152.808	156.11
1979	1	160.053	163.232	167.275	171.714
1980	1	176.719	180.586	184.613	189.164
1981	1	193.24			

		Per Capita	Hours Worked	Per Week	
1948	1	24.4081	24.5651	24.5377	24.4427
1949	1	23.9676	23.7894	23.3321	23.3202
1950	1	23.3794	23.6307	24.0283	24.0508
1951	1	24.3355	24.3792	24.5267	24.219
1952	1	24.4683	24.1751	24.0549	24.3893
1953	1	24.5186	24.2007	24.1054	23.7828
1954	1	23.4174	23.0957	22.859	22.9464
1955	1	23.3124	23.3365	23.8715	23.9023
1956	1	23.9133	23.9242	23.9617	23.8341
1957	1	23.7526	23.5422	23.472	23.0542
1958	1	22.5518	22.4383	22.4046	22.7434
1959	1	22.7784	23.046	22.8695	22.7777
1960	1	22.6122	23.0295	22.9992	22.7056
1961	1	22.5141	22.3225	22.312	22.5442
1962	1	22.5202	22.6517	22.5588	22.4623
1963	1	22.394	22.5329	22.4491	22.4778
1964	1	22.3338	22.6493	22.4657	22.5526
1965	1	22.7423	22.8232	22.8428	23.0068
1966		22.9991	23.0685	23.0833	23.098
1967		23.0906	23.0241	23.2083	23.2011
1968	1	23.0192	23.1808	23.209	23.1812
1969	1	23.1054	23.2199	23.2648	23.181
1970	1	22.9715	22.8039	22.6012	22.4735
1971	1	22.3341	22.2897	22.1942	22.3522
1972	1	22.3958	22.4593	22.5155	22.5196
1973	1	22.6198	22.8116	22.8589	22.9457
1974	1	22.8261	22.7511	22.6516	22.3101
1975		21.7893	21.6395	21.6866	21.8196
1976	1	22.0321	22.0682	22.0907	22.1806
1977	1	22.2424	22.5613	22.5659	22.7518
1978	1	22.8953	23.4821	23.232	23.4287
1979		23.5041	23.4095	23.4278	23.5442
1980	1	23.3296	22.828	22.6608	22.8242
1981	1	22.9808			

After Tax Compensation of Nonagricultural Employees

Year					
1947	1	1.05326	1.10046	1.13768	1.18948
1948	1	1.21603	1.23419	1.27342	1.29148
1949	1	1.30153	1.31132	1.31423	1.31586
1950	1	1.33078	1.33066	1.34682	1.37884
1951	1	1.40515	1.43341	1.451	1.47696
1952	1	1.49488	1.51599	1.53447	1.55827
1953	1	1.56917	1.5982	1.61918	1.62939
1954	1	1.65201	1.66946	1.68607	1.69902
1955	1	1.70366	1.71949	1.74195	1.76021
1956	1	1.7821	1.81156	1.83736	1.85406
1957	1	1.88364	1.9061	1.92462	1.94462
1958		1.9576	1.98855	2.02892	2.03
1959	1	2.04334	2.05373	2.06949	2.08253
1960		2.11673	2.13069	2.13757	2.14798
1961	1	2.16017	2.16996	2.18371	2.2094
1962		2.24817	2.25636	2.26386	2.27576
1963	1	2.28977	2.29257	2.31895	2.37195
1964		2.44614	2.48961	2.54119	2.5627
1965	1	2.56812	2.59016	2.61571	2.64181
1966	1	2.66183	2.6933	2.7381	2.76705
1967	1	2.80463	2.83	2.85374	2.87796
1968	1	2.91771	2.94134	2.96778	3.00251
1969	1	3.03294	3.07656	3.14362	3.20135
1970	1	3.26616	3.34898	3.4403	3.44999
1971	1	3.52528	3.57353	3.62174	3.65462
1972	1	3.75025	3.78711	3.83014	3.8815
1973	1	3.95776	3.98998	4.03862	4.11371
1974	1	4.18268	4.29485	4.38762	4.4963
1975	1	4.61002	4.6968	4.78804	4.87599
1976	1	4.96132	5.07213	5.14693	5.24567
1977	1	5.33795	5.42641	5.50795	5.61742
1978	1	5.71794	5.79717	5.90583	6.03649
1979	1	6.1863	6.34586	6.43757	6.59069
1980	1	6.71842	6.87616	7.03934	7.23279

After Tax Nominal Interest Rate on Treasury Bills

Year					
1947	1	1.00066	1.00066	1.00126	1.00158
1948	1	1.00172	1.00174	1.00181	1.00198
1949	1	1.00203	1.00202	1.00178	1.00187
1950	1	1.00195	1.00203	1.00215	1.00236
1951	1	1.00244	1.00267	1.00284	1.00287
1952	1	1.00286	1.00292	1.00319	1.00335
1953	1	1.00356	1.00383	1.00352	1.00259
1954	1	1.00189	1.00142	1.00152	1.00181
1955	1	1.00219	1.00264	1.00324	1.00409
1956	1	1.00414	1.00451	1.00451	1.00532
1957	1	1.0055	1.00548	1.00587	1.0058
1958	1	1.0032	1.00178	1.00298	1.00484
1959	1	1.00486	1.00524	1.00613	1.00744
1960		1.00683	1.00537	1.00416	1.00411
1961	1	1.00413	1.00404	1.00404	1.0043
1962	1	1.00476	1.00472	1.00496	1.00487
1963	1	1.00505	1.00511	1.00569	1.00607
1964	1	1.00613	1.00604	1.00608	1.00639
1965		1.00676	1.00672	1.00669	1.0072
1966	1	1.00801	1.00795	1.00872	1.00906
1967	1	1.00784	1.00634	1.00752	1.00827
1968	1	1.00875	1.00951	1.00902	1.00963
1969	1	1.01057	1.01075	1.01211	1.01257
1970	1	1.01247	1.01161	1.01097	1.00925
1971	1	1.00669	1.00728	1.00872	1.00733
1972	1	1.00596	1.0065	1.00734	1.00838
1973	1	1.00973	1.01137	1.01437	1.01281
1974		1.01304	1.01416	1.0142	1.0126
1975	1	1.01012	1.00932	1.01091	1.0098
1976	1	1.00856	1.00892	1.00892	1.00812
1977	1	1.008	1.00834	1.00944	1.01057
1978		1.01103	1.01115	1.01256	1.01486
1979	1	1.01599	1.01601	1.01644	1.02005
1980	1	1.02276	1.01714	1.01578	1.02317
1981	1	1.02425			

CPSIA information can be obtained
at www.ICGtesting.com
Printed in the USA
BVHW04s1001100418
512972BV00021B/443/P